Budgeting Is Crap

It causes stress, anxiety and sleepless nights.
Learn The Alternative Solution To Not Flush Your
Money Away

• • •

By Samantha Boardman

Publisher information and year

ISBN-13: 978-0-6487050-0-0

Copyright © Samantha Boardman 2019

The right of Samantha Boardman to be identified as the author of this work has been asserted by her in accordance with the Copyright, Designs and Patents Act 1988

All rights reserved. No part of this publication may be reproduced, stored in a retrieval system, or transmitted, in any form, or by any means (electronic, mechanical, photocopying, recording or otherwise) without the prior written permission of the publisher.

Designations used by companies to distinguish their products are often claimed as trademarks. All brand names and product names used in this book are trade names, service marks, trademarks or registered trademarks of their respective owners. The publisher is not associated with any product or vendor mentioned in this book. This publication is designed to provide accurate and authoritative information in regard to the subject matter covered. It is sold on the understanding that the publisher is not engaged in rendering professional services. If professional advice or other expert assistance is required, the services of a competent professional should be sought.

This book is sold subject to the condition that it shall not, by way of trade or otherwise, be lent, hired out, or otherwise circulated without the publisher's prior consent in any form of binding or cover other than that in which it is published and without a similar condition including this condition being imposed on the subsequent purchaser.

This is dedicated to:

Saki, the smartest and bestest police dog in the world.

Table of Contents

Foreword	9
Disclaimer	10
Chapter 1 Budgeting with 10 Pence	11
Chapter 2 My Parents Charged Me Rent: It Changed My Life	19
Chapter 3 Budgeting Ruined My Life	27
Chapter 4 Credit Is A Nightmare	35
Chapter 5 Frequencies Are A Killer	43
Chapter 6 Special Occasions	49
Chapter 7 Spending Mindsets	57
Chapter 8 Why A Spending Plan Is The Answer	65
Chapter 9 Spending Made Easy: Success Stories	69
Chapter 10 Spending Worksheet	77

Foreword

The Beginning

This book has been written by Spending Planner Expert, Samantha Boardman and is her own account of her personal budgeting experiences growing up, and the financial decisions that she made along the way. It starts with her very first "finance/budget related" memory as a child and then takes you through all of the ever changing financial challenges that life throws at us all, on an ongoing basis.

She has always Budgeted (in one way, or another) and has always been very organised. All of the jobs she ever had involved being very structured and co-ordinated with a certain amount of logistics and forward thinking included. That hasn't changed now that she has her own Business; Spending Made Easy. Quite the opposite in fact. With her business, she takes the stress out of the day to day finances and has proven that the "traditional style" of budgeting is (well and truly) out, and that Spending Plans are in! Spending Plans are 100% more effective than traditional styles of budgeting.

Disclaimer:

This book is not a source of financial advice. This book is Samantha Boardman's budgeting and spending life story. The information in this book is based on her own personal opinion and life experiences. It should not be considered as professional financial advice. The ideas and strategies should never be used without first assessing your own personal and financial situation, or without consulting a financial professional. Her thoughts and opinions will also change from time to time as she learns and accumulates more knowledge.

For further information

www.SpendingMadeEasy.com.au

Budgeting With 10 Pence

Chapter 1

Right then, where do I start? I am often asked how long I have been Budgeting for and where I learnt to budget. The fact of the matter is that I have ALWAYS budgeted. Haven't we All? Whether we do it poorly or nail it, we are all Budgeting in some form or another.

My very first memory of Budgeting is when I was a little girl... The newspaper used to be 8 Pence (I grew up in England, hence the 8 pence – "Great British Pence"). I would be given 10 pence by my Father to go and get the evening newspaper. As I was actually doing a chore, the extra 2 pence was my payment. Whooppee! I could go and choose what I wanted to spend my 2 pence on. Being a young girl, it would always be sweets (Whoops - Lollies!). I could get 4 lollies for 2 pence. Bargain, and well worth the effort of the walk to and from our local newsagent.

On the walk I would also take the dog (bonus point for taking him for a walk). I used to love walking the dog. He was a Police Dog, called Saki. I would plead with him to sit and wait outside the shop and he did so regularly. Taking instructions from a child as if his life depended on it. He was so obedient.

One day, when I came out of the shop with the newspaper, and my 4 lollies, he was gone! Disappeared! I was only in there a few minutes buying the trusty newspaper and he had managed to escape.

After about an hour of searching for poor lost Saki, I headed home with the newspaper, and no dog! What would the Police say? I had lost a Police dog! Saki used to love carrying the newspaper home for his real Master; my Father. He didn't even get it wet in his mouth. He was that gentle (not if you were a criminal though) and he won many awards. Saki was fabulous and I always considered him my best friend.

Anyway… on this particular day, I walked home without Saki, scared to death of what my Father would say. As I began to blubber and confess what had happened, I was advised that Saki had been home over half an hour! Damn you clever, obedient Police Dog, with excellent navigational skills! That day I didn't particularly enjoy my 4 lollies but I had brought the newspaper back in one piece and so I had earned them. That is my very first memory of budgeting.

I guess I didn't know at the time what I was really doing. All I knew was that I was "allowed" to keep the 2 pence for going to the shop in the first place.

When I was a little older, I wanted a horse. A Palomino Pony to be exact. I just loved the biscuit colour of the coat, white mane, and tail. They were the most beautiful things on the planet as far as I was concerned and so I just had to have one. As any child does as they are growing up, I nagged (and nagged and nagged) my parents about wanting my Pony. I neeeeeeeeded a pony.

As with any pet, I of course promised to take care of it, look after it, feed it and ride it every day. No matter how nicely I asked, or how many times I tried to work my cute little girl charm, no-one was going to buy me a pony. Many Christmases and Birthdays came and went, and there was never a Palomino gift wrapped for me to open.

Being a kid with no money sucked sometimes as I wanted and needed many things, but could never afford them. In this case, I had to figure out what I was going to do to ensure that a Pony, and a Palomino one at that, entered my life. I did get pocket money, but I wasn't convinced it would be enough. So, I did my research, even if it was just to prove how keen I really was, and I found out how much a Palomino Pony cost.

I was shocked.

I was sad.

Disappointed like never before.

I could not afford the Pony all by myself.

It was heart wrenching….

No one wanted to buy me one and I couldn't afford one. But I had to have one! So… I had a chat with my Father about what I should do to get the money I needed, so that I could buy the damn thing myself. Do you know what he said? He said that if I bought the pony myself, that he would pay for its upkeep.

Giddy (see what I did there?) with excitement that I could get a pony, off I went to research how much he was willing to cough up! I found out how much stabling ("agistment") cost, food, vets bills, saddles, reigns, rugs, horse shoes, etc…. It was not a cheap animal to keep, let me tell you… However, I was motivated by the fact that my Father was prepared to lay out ALL of this, on an ongoing basis, IF (and it was a big "if"), I bought the pony myself, in the first place.

Little did my Father know how much I wanted the Palomino Pony. All I had to do was to find the money to buy one outright!

"The idea of a pony is fun,
but the ongoing bills that come with it, are not so much fun"

Samantha Boardman

Easy! Then all my prayers would be answered. He had no idea who he was dealing with. My Father was pretty smug with the deal he had made with me, his youngest child. He reckoned he was safe and that I would NOT, and more importantly could NOT save up the money to buy the pony. That was like a red rag to a bull to me! How wrong he was... I was a determined, stubborn little thing. Always thinking outside the box.

So! Now I knew how much one was, I decided it would take me a few years to save up, and if I did enough "jobs around the house", it might only take 3 to 4 years. I did my sums, and made a fabulous chart of all my future payments that would result in me purchasing the pony outright. I broke it down into weeks so that I had an exact payment (savings!) plan to work to. I transferred all of these details onto a bright piece of blue cardboard and pinned it to my bedroom wall all hand-written.

This marvellous, problem solving piece of blue cardboard was on my wall, on the right-hand side as you went into my bedroom. At eye level so that I could see it every time I entered and left my bedroom to remind me. Just the focus I needed. I could "see" the Palomino in my sights... This was in the days before laminators were invented and so I carefully covered it with clear tape so that it wouldn't fray, or fade (or at least I thought so).... No matter what, I had a plan - and little did I know, it was my very first Spending Plan (but more of that later).

The weeks, months and years soon passed and I was following the plan to the tee! I was often ahead if I had been a really good and busy girl.

If I remember rightly, it took me about 3 to 4 years to reach my financial goal and I was thrilled when I had enough money to buy myself my Palomino Pony. However! That joy was not shared by my Father as he was quaking in his boots at this stage as he (clearly) didn't believe that I would save enough money for my beloved Pony. He even ridiculed me along the way. Surely he knew how stubborn and determined I was? Thinking back, perhaps the teasing was a sabotage attempt? Silly man.

The thing is, as the years went by, I actually went off the idea of having a pony. I still kept my focus and drive though, as I knew there would be something to spend my money on, at some point in my life. I must succeed at what I had set out to do – that is Me – the stubborn youngest child.

At this stage in my life, I was about 16 years old and having a pony was "so last year", so I bought myself a car, a bright blue Mini 850 instead. My very first little car! A cool blue one, and I could not have been happier. Way more fun than a pony, but "neigh", the car had more seats and more horsepower.

My Father was delighted; as you could imagine.

Budgeting Is Crap

My Parents Charged Me Rent: It Changed My Life

Chapter 2

So here I was, the sixteen year old (or thereabouts), living at home with my parents and a car owner too. Whoohoo! Life didn't get any better than this! To say my Father was relieved that he didn't have to pay for the upkeep of a potential four-legged Palomino Pony friend is an understatement. However, I think he realised only then, just how stubborn I could be.

I had left school at 16 and thought I could chill at home whilst I figured out what I was going to do with my life. I wasn't a big fan of school and the only subjects I liked were Mathematics and Art. Plus, to "stay on" at school meant you had to do more exams; something I had never been very good at. So I took my chances in the big, bad, world and left school. Summer holidays, here I come!

As I had never been very good at knowing what I wanted to do, I took the Summer off to decide. Summer came and went and I still had no clue what I was going to do with my life. There I was with my little, blue Mini 850, and nowhere to go in it.

I was forced by my parents to do a YTS (Youth Training Scheme), which was kind of like work experience, but for "grown-ups". To say "forced" might be a harsh word, but it certainly felt like it at the time. My Mother worked for Shell UK Oil and they needed participants for their YTS at School Leaver age. My Mother dutifully signed me up for this and so then I had no choice. I was going to work at Shell UK, Monday to Friday from 9am till 5pm and only get a measly 25 Pounds (England remember!) per week. Slave labour, I thought.

It wasn't all bad, there were some benefits to be had in doing the YTS and so I went along – but only because I had nothing better to do with my life. I also wasn't allowed to stay at home without a job after the School Summer Holidays had finished. In my eyes at the age of 16, this felt unfair as I wanted time to think about what I wanted to do, but it had been months and I felt lost.

Essentially, I was offered the option of going back to school or the YTS. School included exams and I knew I was never any good at those. I did get good grades, but they were never great! So, YTS Shell UK it was. Joy! Somewhere to go in my cute little Mini – all bought and paid for. That was a stroke of luck, wasn't it, as I wasn't going to get very far on 25 Pounds per week! That is about AU$ 45 per week, which is very rough to live on. I am sure you can agree.

Despite me not really knowing what I was doing with my life, or why I was there, I enjoyed my time at Shell and still have friends I made to this day, some 35+ years on.

At this point, my Parents had advised me that I had to "do something" (with my life) if I wanted to stay living at home. They advised me that as soon as I started earning, I must start contributing to the household. Really? Not only was I working for peanuts, I was having to give some of my hard-earned pay to my Parents! Who didn't need the money anyway! Let's face it, they were already paying the mortgage and the bills. Why on earth would they charge their own children to live in a house that they had always lived in? Rude.

Pretty much like me nagging for the pony, me nagging that I didn't want to pay "rent" (board, keep; whatever you want to call it) fell on deaf ears. Each time I got my 25 pounds on a Friday afternoon, which ironically was handed out by my own Mother half the time, I had to go home and immediately (and when I say immediately, I mean immediately) hand over 5 pounds for my board and lodgings. Now, for all that slave labour, I was only getting 20 Pounds per week. It was daylight robbery in my opinion, and so very rude of my Parents to take my cash when I didn't have very much of it in the first place.

They were both earning good money. They didn't need MY money. I distinctly remember my Father saying; "you will thank me one day". He would go on and on about how important it is to contribute to the household. He even admitted that they didn't even need my money, and that it was all about teaching me that you have to pay your way in this world. More importantly, you had to pay your bills first – then you can spend the rest.

As time went on, after about 6 months to be exact, I got a proper job with an insurance company and so I got a proper wage to go with it. Whoohoo. I was so excited. I had a job, a real one, in the heart of Manchester City Centre and I loved it. I thought that I would make (or do I mean save?) loads of money as the 5 Pounds per week "rent" would be a lot easier to manage as there would be more spare cash. My new job was paying me way more than the 25 pounds per week I was getting at Shell UK. Marvellous!

As I started to plan what to do with the extra cash from my fabulous new job, in swooped my Parents with the dreaded news. You know what I am going to say, right? That the rent was going up. I was advised that 5 Pounds was "nothing" and that it was time to increase it in line with my earnings. Once again, I felt like I was being cheated. Robbed by my own Parents! It appeared to me, that as soon as I got any money whatsoever, there were my Parents, my Father in particular,

"Don't kick your kids out of home, charge them rent and then they will go voluntarily"

Samantha Boardman

standing there with his hand out, waiting for me to pay him... He didn't even need the money! Policemen were paid very well in those days. So annoying! How was I ever going to get ahead, save any money, move out, upgrade my trusty Mini 850 with him around?

As time went on, the rent went up and up (and up and up)... In fact, it went up so high that I could no longer afford to live there. Yes! You heard me right, the rent went up so much that I could not afford to live in my own family home. In my own house! Once again, my Father uttered those words to me; "you will thank me one day". Geeze that was annoying. All I could see was that he was hindering any chances of me going anywhere with my life.

As stubborn Samantha (now in my early 20s), I moaned on and on about how hard done by I was. He had a response, of course he did! My Father educated me and very categorically detailed to me the costs involved in the upkeep of a house. Mortgage, Gas, Electric, Food, Insurance, Rates, etc... The list went on. How would I have known all of that? I had never been a home owner. I had to do something...

I had nowhere else to go, as I had only ever lived at home, but the rent I was paying to my Parents was so high! I devised a plan. If I detailed what it would cost ME to move out, and thus prove to them that I could not afford to move out, then they would have to let me stay, right? My older brother and sister both had moved out after marrying their long-term childhood sweethearts and so there was just one kid left at home. Me. The stubborn one.

Once again, I did my research on the cost of living out-of-home. I found out how much the living expenses were for a small apartment/unit/flat. I didn't even look at "real" houses as I knew that was way out of my reach. I eventually established my estimated potential costs for gas, electric, mortgage (or rent!), rates, insurances, car loan (yes, the trusty Mini 850 was traded in for a red Ford Fiesta), my "going out money" (ever so important, that one), petrol, and of course my clothes money. When it was all added together, it was WAY more than what I earnt – even at my fabulous, high paying job in the heart of Manchester. What was I to do?

My plan to show my Parents how expensive living out-of-home was, was now in place and so I approached my Father with my dilemma. Surely when he saw how much things cost (as if he didn't know already, huh?), then he would let me stay – but with cheaper rent. How could he refuse? He wouldn't let his youngest daughter live on the streets, now would he? Surely not? Once again, how wrong I was...

My painful, stubborn, tearful presentation of how I could not afford to move out was met with this sentence; "If you find somewhere else to live, for what you are being asked to pay here, then tell us, and we will all go and live there". As the tears flowed, it dawned on me very quickly, that this man (my Father) was serious. I had to think fast, I had to think quickly, and I had to think outside the box... The more upset I got, the more chance I thought I had of him changing his mind.... Nope! It was never going to happen.

His words of comfort as I sat crying were this; "work it out Sam, work it out. You are not living here forever". So, I had to get my thinking cap on. Pretty quick and smartish too. There was no easing me in gradually, the rent was going up and I was either paying it – on pay day, as always, or I was moving out. Good job I am adaptable and stubborn.

I went back to my trusted research techniques about the cost-of-living and started to think about how I could afford to move out – and in the meantime, the rent increased. I wasn't going to stay where I was clearly not wanted! This charging me rent business opened up my eyes to the many financial commitments that lay ahead of me and my future life. There was no escape. It was very expensive this living malarkey. I was in dire straits, but little did I know that my Parents charging me rent was the best lesson they could have taught me, for my financial future.

Budgeting Ruined My Life

Chapter 3

Thinking, thinking, thinking..... Budgeting had seriously ruined my life! Nothing seemed to fit in it anymore. What was I to do? My trusty Budget; all hand-written on a piece of paper, was just a list with all my outgoings on it. Proof, right there, as clear as day, that I could NOT afford to live anywhere! Where had all these expenses come from?

Some of my friends Parents weren't charging them rent and so of course, my Parents were the worst in the world. For a young lady, living at home, expenses were generally; rent (of course), car loan, fuel, entertainment (my "going out" money), clothes, etc... On top of that, I was always trying to save up for a holiday with my friend, but never succeeding. We loved the idea of going to the Greek Islands and it was always so easy to get a good deal. How was I supposed to enjoy my life if my own Parents were sabotaging my happiness? It appeared to me that I had a lifestyle that I couldn't afford on my budget, so was it really a lifestyle? It was just facts, on a bit of paper. Useless!

After some soul searching and investigative research (again!), it became very clear to me that I needed to get more money, more income! - from somewhere. Anywhere!

As I had a great full time job in the heart of Manchester, I was away from home from 8am until 6pm, Monday to Friday. What spare time in my already busy day, was I supposed to conjure up so that I could free myself up to earn some extra cash? Really? Why did I get the Parents that wanted to teach me a life lesson? Nothing was fair anymore and I was not a happy bunny…..

Until someone told me about catalogues.

If you ran a catalogue, and people ordered stuff from you, then you got commission. All you had to do was hand out a few catalogues that people wanted to buy from and you would get yourself a little earner... I signed up with Grattan Catalogue and started to take it everywhere with me. I often left it on the table in the tearoom at work and people would leave their orders on bits of paper inside it for me. I felt like a right little

"You only grow financially
when you are financially uncomfortable"

Samantha Boardman

entrepreneur bringing everyone's items in each time they had arrived.

Now that I was this budding catalogue entrepreneur, I was constantly asked about the status of an order and if things could be returned or not. This was easy! I "worked" in my lunchtimes and did other catalogue related tasks in the evenings and on weekends... I really enjoyed it, but it wasn't enough.

In fact, I enjoyed it so much though that I took on another catalogue; Freemans. However, the same thing happened... It was good, but it wasn't enough. I had to think of something else... Thinking, thinking... What else could I do?

Ding Dong! Avon Calling...

Avon was yet another catalogue with beauty products for sale that was pretty much door to door mail order. You dropped catalogues off at people's houses and they would order from you (or not). Then you delivered it personally to them the month after (when the huge delivery – of everyone's orders - arrived at your door). I had heaps of fun sorting out everyone's orders on my lounge floor. My partner at the time (let's just call him Ryan), used to help me. We would package it all up and off we would go, delivering the orders to all of our happy customers and getting their payments at the same time. Avon worked on about 20-25% commission at the time and so we only ever had to pay Avon about 80% of what we collected. It was like a little goldmine.

Running all of these catalogues soon resulted in a very large problem. I could not keep up with my orders and Lord only knows how long it would have taken me without Ryan's help. He loved being the cashier! We were a good team, we got lots of orders and ran a pretty great business... but still... you guessed it.... it wasn't enough income. We needed more money!

We even had the option of buying Avon products at seriously discounted prices. It was a perk of being an Avon Rep. We would buy loads of stuff; soaps, bubble baths, makeup, moisturisers, toys, gifts and more. You name it, we bought it and cheap! Very cheap. We used a portion of the commission to buy it with. We would then sit and package it all up into little individual parcels that looked like gift bags and sell them door to door. People would buy a parcel from us, still at a discounted price, but nowhere near the cost that we had paid in the first place. So, we made even more money! It was a "win win" situation; we made even more money and the customers got lots of discounted Avon products at the same time. Fabulous. But guess what? You know what I am going to say here, don't you? It still wasn't enough!

Damn you Parents who are forcing me to do this. I was trying to have a nice life, but I just didn't have the time!

However, I found time... more time... I had to. I found the time to work at a Night Club for three nights per week. Thursday (was student night), Friday, and often a Monday (the oldies – Grab a Granny we used to call it). First of all, I had to get permission from my "real job" in Manchester and they granted it to me, on the condition that it didn't affect my daytime work with them. I needed the money and so I had to make it work.

Working nights at the night club was good, but I was sooooooo tired on the days after the Night Club shift and stifled many a yawn at my desk, ensuring that no one was looking, of course! The best thing about working at a night club is the Tips! I worked at a very "glamourous" club with lots of Actors (from Coronation Street and the like) and there was always a Football Player in there too! They partied hard and tipped well. I made a few celebrity friends and they always looked after me with Tips, because I always looked after them, with my fabulous chatty and friendly customer service – even though I was "dead on my feet" half the time. Ha ha...

These were the days where you could smoke in a Night Club and my lovely, long hair used to always smell of smoke. I hated it. I have never smoked and I just don't "get it". So unhealthy! I stuck at it though, because I needed the money.

I would go out on the odd evening on the weekend with my friends, if I could summon up the energy of course. I would pay for drinks with my Tips – thus not breaking into my bank account. I would spill my bag of coins onto the bar and count out how much I needed for my round of drinks. I even sometimes went to the same club where I worked, as I didn't have to pay to get in then, perk of the job. You see, I was even saving myself money then (the entrance fee was expensive in my glamourous club)... and I got to hang out with my celebrity mates. Fun, but I was exhausted....

The good news was that my bank balance started to look a little healthier and I tried my very hardest to "live off my tips". I didn't always manage it, but I did try. If only there was more money coming in.... God, this living business is tiresome.

Then! A job came up at the local pub. Of course I applied and got it. Here we go again! Serving pub meals on a Saturday lunchtime/afternoon. That was okay as I got to have some sort of "lie in" on a Saturday morning, before I headed off. My bedroom was always full of uniforms – stinking of smoke. I was forever washing – or hanging uniforms outside to get rid of the smell of the smoke. The money was always good at pubs and clubs because if you work Public holidays and Christmas and New Year, etc... they would give you double pay, or something like that anyway.

Working these five jobs, seemed worth it when you went home with more money in your bank account, even when you did stink of smoke and couldn't keep your eyes open. The massive problem though was that the budget that I made was destroying me, big time. I was tired, exhausted and didn't seem to have the time, or the energy to live that fabulous lifestyle that I wanted. I used to dream of only working one job at a time.

Imagine if I had that Palomino Pony too! He would have starved due to neglect, I am sure of it.

Still, all this income did do me some good after all. My plan had finally worked! I managed to scrape together a deposit for the one bedroomed tiny apartment that I bought. It was no bigger than a shoe box. My first home. I painted it myself and was given second-hand furniture whilst I figured out a way to save for my new stuff. Being the youngest, I always dreamt of having new stuff, instead of my sister's "hand me downs". I even managed to find the time to paint the walls myself. I am tired just thinking about all this again.

However, I now had to keep going to keep up with the mortgage repayments. The biggest financial commitment of my life.

Credit Is A Nightmare

Chapter 4

Credit! Credit cards..... I was eligible for a credit card. Welcome to adulthood Samantha! When it became apparent to me what a credit card would and could do to solve my money shortfalls, I was ecstatic. How cool! You could acquire things with a piece of plastic and then pay for it later on. Whoever invented this magnificent system was a genius. All my Prayers had been answered.

However, I was always very careful with my Credit Card as I was aware (as I always do my research BEFOREHAND, remember?) that the interest rate was high; but only if you didn't pay your balance off in full each month. I did my own investigations and my maths and factored all of this into my budget and, if I am totally honest, it did make my life a little easier. I always dealt with the facts first and managed my finances quite well. Juggling all of these jobs, catalogues, Avon, and working in the City; the credit card just helped me a little. I always knew that I had to pay for it in the end.

I was only able to achieve this financial harmony because I was brought up in a household where, if you couldn't afford it, you didn't have it; end of story. Being the youngest of 3 children, and my sister being only 11 months older than me, I lived in her "hand me downs". I got her clothes, her shoes. I even got her old bike once – as a Christmas present! I always promised myself that when I earnt my own money, that I would buy everything brand new – Myself. With my own money. I would save up for it first, then go out and buy it! Whatever it was... My, how times have changed.

These days, we are in the "NOW" economy. You can have literally anything you want and pay for it later. The problem is, we live in a high consuming society and there is a plethora of wants... while our needs such as rent/mortgage, bills, food, etc... are not being satisfied. People will often use there last few dollars on a "want" and sacrifice a "need" to get it.

A good example of satisfying a want first over a need is the decision to buy a packet of cigarettes with your last $20 rather than buying dinner. The craving for the cigarette is fulfilled but the hunger that is life giving, is not.

"Destroy your credit card before your credit card destroys you"

Samantha Boardman

Satisfying any want using a credit card can then lead to chasing the interest payments and ending up paying more than if you saved up for it in the first place. Furthermore, during the saving time, you have time to reflect on whether you actually need the item, rather than want it. A bit like if I bought my Palomino Pony instead of my car. This is similar to Buyer's Remorse.

Buyer's Remorse, is essentially when people do not think about the ramifications of impulse purchases, which can leave them without their "needs". They see it, they want it, they can have it now. Psychological studies have proven that impulse purchases can release serotonin. This a feeling of happiness and that is why we love doing it again and again. It's a feeling of being able to have it "now" (happy), and then we see the credit card bill later (unhappy).

For some people, there is a belief that they don't have to pay for their impulse purchases as credit cards do not have a tangible aspect compared to the many dollar notes an item could cost.

In contrast, when you take out a mortgage or a loan with a bank, they go through all the repayments with you. They even do their own financial checks on you (and with you) to ensure that THEY are happy that YOU can repay the loan. None of this due diligence is going on for ourselves when we see that shiny object, or that fabulous pair of shoes that we just have to have; whether we can afford them, or not…. We don't lay out all the repayments in front of ourselves, and see the affect it has on our financial situation BEFORE we commit. We just commit.

The trusty credit card is there… burning a hole in your pocket, ready for us to have that fabulous feeling of "it's mine, all mine". Plus! The Sales Assistants in the shops are only too happy to upsell you, or offer you the same thing in a different colour. How many times have you heard "why don't you get them both"? From a sales assistant – or even worse - a friend! When was the last time you went to a fast food restaurant and asked for a burger only to have them say would you like fries with that? Do we ever say no? It's only a few dollars, but a few dollars again and again over a year adds up.

These days, it's not just Credit Cards. We also have; Buy Now – Pay Later, Interest Free Credit, Rent to Own and more. All of these fabulous services are allowing us to give ourselves permission to have all those "wants"… even if we only half want them. It is a well-known fact that we are more likely to spend more on a purchase, if there is credit offered at the time of shopping, because it is low commitment. So that $100 pair of jeans that you had your eye on, suddenly turns into a $200 pair of jeans and you can walk out of the shop with your fabulous new purchase, without parting with any of your hard earned cash. In that transaction, we never consider the repayments or interest, just that instant gratification that we so crave.

Back in my day – the days when I was saving for my Palomino Pony – credit wasn't so readily available. If I wanted a $100 pair of jeans, I had to save up for the $100 pair of jeans and the shop didn't give me them, unless I handed over my $100 at the time of purchase. That was the same with all of my purchases. My, how times have changed! These days, we are living in a cashless society, and a "I can have it now" society and no-one, as far as I can see, is warning us of the ramifications and pitfalls of the financial commitment that we are entering into. Most importantly, no one warns you of the COST that ultimately, you are going to pay, which is all going to happen in the future.

As a result of this indulgent lifestyle, we are all getting what we want, when we want it, and getting ourselves deeper and deeper into debt – without even thinking about it, or often realising it. The sad thing is... we really don't seem to care either.

The younger generation who are surrounded by this indulgent credit environment don't know any different and so this is the norm to them. They grew up with it. As Budgeting (or should I say Spending?) is not taught in schools, where is that going to get them? It is a scary thought. When I was growing up it wasn't taught in schools either, but thanks to my Father, I was forced to deal with the facts. I had to, and I did my own research. As we know, I even had my own Father put the rent up each time I got a sniff of any pay increase, I had to learn how to spend wisely, and I had to learn quick.

Spending wisely wasn't about having more income coming in. A tweak here and there was very beneficial.... Not going out every week with my friends, cutting back on my shoes and clothing purchases every now and then. It all made a difference! What do they say? "Take care of the pennies and the pounds will take care of themselves"...

These days everyone is spending a lot and not even thinking about it. Things have to change, and the main thing is mindset. People's mindset around Spending is not what it should be. Don't get me wrong, I have no issues with Credit Cards, Buy Now – Pay Later, etc, etc...

- If YOU do your research and KNOW the future repayments before you commit.

- If YOU can afford those repayments, for as long as they are due (you know, like your mortgage, or your car loan).

- If YOU can pay them ON time, EVERY time, then certainly – go ahead and make the purchase.

However, today's environment and the cashless society is encouraging us all to spend all of our money – and more, before we even have it in our pockets, without thinking about having to pay for it all, in the future.

Frequencies Are A Killer

Chapter 5

One of the things that used to do my head in when I was budgeting as I was growing up, was the fact that there is not four weeks in every month. Especially, when I had all my expenses written out on my piece of paper, I based it on one month, as I was always paid monthly. Strangely, every proper job I had growing up (apart from my 6 months as a YTS Trainee) I was paid monthly and so I was always a Monthly Girl. I always knew the amount of pay I was going to get monthly, so that was where I started. In those days, a lot of my bills and expenses were monthly anyway, until I got more homeowner related expenses after I bought my first home.

However! Being a young girl who generally only went out on a weekend, I used to count the weekends. No, I am not kidding.

Realising there were often five weekends that fell between my monthly pay cycles was devastating, as you can imagine. Each month, I would either divide the monthly amount by four, or sometimes five. A five weekend month would hurt as it would significantly lower the amount I could spend. Could you imagine how much of a difference that made to my going out money?

Each month I would take my monthly pay, account for all of the monthly deductions and pay them accordingly... then, the "going out money" had to be either split four ways, or even worse; five ways! I can distinctly remember the monthly going out money being one hundred pounds (England remember). A lot of the months were four weekends long and so I had twenty five pounds to spend. Happy Days... When the month had five weekends in it, the going out money reduced to twenty pounds per weekend. That five pounds difference, although seems small, was significant as this could have paid for another drink, or my cab fare home.

I used to fit a lot of spending in to that twenty or twenty five pounds, but Sod's Law always occurred. I always seemed to need more money on those busier weekends, which were often on the weekend of the five weekends in a month. It was a nightmare.

To combat the five weekends a month, I used to attempt to pretend that there were five weekends in every month because

"The fact that there are five weeks in some months makes budgeting even harder"

Samantha Boardman

I thought that might be easier, and then there would be excess cash when there was only four weekends. This however became way too complicated for my simple brain. In the end, the end of the month came around quick and I always seemed to spend all of my money, no matter how many weekends there were in it. Damn it. This Budgeting malarkey was not much fun when I was growing up and attempting to pay for all of my financial commitments wasn't working. Adulting was hard!

Once I became a homeowner (albeit a VERY small unit, that I lovingly called "home"), all of those home owning obligatory expenses came into play. Expenses such as gas, electric, phone (landline in those days), mortgage, rates, council tax. Not to mention all of the expenses that I had gotten used to when I lived "at home"; petrol, car loan, going out money, clothes, and more.

As I got older, the frequencies became more varied. I was attempting to pay for things, quarterly, monthly, annually. It was a flipping nightmare to keep up. I kept having to go back to my monthly pay to attempt to squeeze it all in. It never used to fit in and I had to earn more to live. I was forever working out an annual amount for something, and then dividing it by twelve so that I could account for it in my monthly budget... Sometimes, there was not enough to cover it all (even with all my side hustles) and so something had to give. Often my clothes money, or even worse, my going out money. If only there was a system that did all of the predicting for me. It would have saved me a lot of time, and energy. If I only knew then, what I know now….. Isn't hindsight marvellous?

Special Occasions

Chapter 6

Another memory from my childhood was Christmas! That goes without saying though, huh? Every kid remembers Christmas. Only I would remember it for different reasons... Other than the traditional fabulous presents and food, our family used to enjoy going out for lunch on Christmas Day. Having someone else cook and serve you delicious food was just too tempting to resist. Not to mention no washing up! It was worth it for that fact alone!

When we ate at home washing up was horrible. Did anyone else argue with their siblings about whose turn it was to wash up? I have an older Brother and Sister, so there were always the three of us to share the chores. We had; wash, dry and "put away". As "put away" was the easiest job, the person who got that, had to make everyone a tea (or coffee). Genius! Imagine the washing and cleaning up involved with 5 "adults" on Christmas Day! As soon as someone suggested we went out, we were all over it! Didn't need asking twice, that was for sure. Especially as we were all getting older, we were all at an age where we would behave ourselves in restaurants!

We lived near Manchester Airport, which meant that there was a very nice and prestigious selection of hotels to choose from. The world was our Oyster!

There was only one flaw in the idea of going to a restaurant on Christmas Day – the expense! These fabulous hotels were quite expensive, and even more so on Christmas Day! They did of course have to pay their staff extra, etc, etc, so it was only to be expected... But it was all worth it! No washing up! No arguing! No having to set the table with all the decorations and crackers, and the like. It was all done for you! How could you not want to?

So! My family of five did this for a few years. We even went to the same Hotel a few times and so became regulars (at Christmas time!). Me being me noticed that the cost was always expensive and when you factored in taxis and the like, it became a very, very expensive lunch. Despite the expense, going out for Christmas lunch is SO worth it – it was in those days anyway! Trust me.

"Special Occasions should be joyful,
not financially regretful"

Samantha Boardman

Guess what I did? Yes! You guessed it... I created a Spending Plan. I found out what the hotel was going to charge; and if I didn't know, I would guess, and then add on a few (Great British) Pounds. Then I would estimate the cost of taxis and any other incidentals; like the fact you cannot get five adults in one taxi and so you would need two!

So! I knew that there was 52 weeks in a year and I also had my "cost per head" for the Christmas Lunch already worked out. These were the two contributing factors that I needed to use to work out how much each family member had to give me – each week, so that they did not get slugged with a huge shock when it came to paying the bills on the day.

I bought myself a little notebook, listed all the weeks of the year in it and added everyone's names and the amount they had to give me – each week – so that they were on track to having enough cash to have a fabulous time on our Christmas Day Outing!

Now then! Not everyone was a fan of my idea – and that was okay. Participating was not compulsory. However, the majority of my family contributed as and when they could. I had people ahead and often behind, but they always knew what they had to do for them to catch up. The ones that didn't participate would get their names in the book too; just as a reminder to me – and them – that they weren't contributing.

Special Occasions

I used to love asking everyone for money and then ticking their amounts off against their names... I felt needed when my family asked me how much they owed etc... It was serving a purpose with my love of organising and budgeting people. It was like running my own little business. Little did I know, huh?

As you can imagine, Christmas Day came and we had all the funds we needed, to pay the hotel lunch bill, pay for any extras (wine, tips and the like), and our taxis to, and from the hotel. Any surplus (because I always over estimated) would be either shared out equally, or put towards the next year. I thought I was a genius. My family knew I loved doing it and so left me to it. I guess there was a certain amount of trust there too. I always put the money in a separate bank account (or Building Society in those days) and so we often had a little bit of interest too! That account was never to be touched. Not only was it NOT my money, but it was set aside for one purpose, and one purpose only; Christmas Day Lunch!

This approach can be adopted for any occasion; including Christmas presents. I know as times have changed, families and friends don't seem to buy each other extravagant gifts anymore, they chose to do other stuff (still costing money though!). However, no matter what you chose to do, you are generally going to have an increase in your spending around Christmas time. Lots of people do all their shopping on Christmas Eve, others choose to do it over the course of the previous twelve months (I seriously take my hat off to you, if you are one of those), or they do the whole lot in around November time.

If we all estimated what we were going to spend at Christmas and then adjusted our day to day spending accordingly throughout the year, we could potentially hardly notice the extravagance of it all; because we planned ahead! Now, correct me if I am wrong, but Christmas is the same time every year, is it not? How many of us (you need to know that I am including myself here), do not account for the added expense that Christmas brings – every, single, year? We all walk around stunned, shocked, buying stuff on impulse that we don't really need (or want), just because it is Christmas. We all know that we can pay for it later with various payment solutions already mentioned in this book; Credit Card, Buy Now – Pay later, etc, etc... you know the drill. More debt, more impulse purchases, more voices in our head telling us we can have it all NOW, and then "worry about that later".

This is the exact same scenario for all of our other regular/annual expenses where we like to treat others; Birthdays, Anniversaries, Easter, Valentine's Day, and more. With a good Spending Plan, we could prevent the overspending, not going overdrawn and it will even remind us that we need to make these purchases. You would never forget anyone's Birthday again!

Special Occasions

Special occasions don't need to creep up on us – they are at the same time every year and we can just slot everything right in, where it belongs, in a Spending Plan, without any of the financial stress that used to go with it.

In a nutshell, ANY expense that you incur in your life is included in your Spending Plan and it will always tell you how much money you need to have in your bank account, at any one time, to keep you on track. As long as you are covering that amount financially, then Happy Days!

Budgeting Is Crap

Spending Mindset

Chapter 7

Spending Mindset (and planning) is what it is all about. This is why I founded my business; Spending Made Easy. It is what I do. I help people with their spending. We are always spending, whether it be on our rent, mortgage, bills, on a daily coffee, or a weekly food shop. Spending is happening all the time. We need to spend to survive.

The most interesting concept of it all is that you are spending when you are saving. If you put a certain amount away each week as savings, then that money is spent too. It might be in your Savings Account, but you should consider it spent; and thus, not available. If we all organised our spending better, and this is my humble opinion, we would not get into the huge amount of debt that today's society is encouraging us to.

Many people use banking Apps or even have a fabulous spreadsheet, but that is often just not enough. Plus, these methods are generally based on historic costs and events, when it is the future that we should be planning for. What is done is done. We need to find out what our future commitments are, and then plan accordingly. This is how a Spending Plan came about.

A Spending Plan tells you exactly how much money you need to have in your bank account NOW – or at any one time in the future. You can see your financial future before you get there. A bit like my Palomino Pony chart; only much more sophisticated.

People need support, guidance, motivation, ideas, comfort, accountability etc... Someone to help with their research and implementation. In some cases people need help wiping their tears away if it has all become too much for them. And we shouldn't be surprised either! Hopefully I have explained why I think that Society's spending is the way it is. Lots of people are overspending and often sadly, without even realising it.

When we achieve all of our Spending Goals, then we also need someone on our side to celebrate with us too. That is what a Spending Planner does.

"Money is a wild beast,
become a Beast Master and control it"

Samantha Boardman

Spending Made Easy was founded in July 2016 after I recognised the need to help others with their Spending Plans. As such, Spending Made Easy is committed to helping people with their spending and their spending habits. As the years in business grew it was established that the core of my business was to take the stress out of our day-to-day finances and to help people become a wise spender. This is knowing where every cent is, and even more importantly, know what you need to have in your bank account at any one time. Having a Spending Plan reduces stress, helps you sleep better at night and might even help you to stop arguing with your partner over money. It is a visual representation of your current financial situation and can project into the future by up to 10 years.

There are 5 core Facts around Spending Made Easy.

1. There is no Shame

There is absolutely no shame in asking for help. Money and finances are such a delicate matter. When people get into difficulty, a lot of the time it is not their fault, they can often bury their heads in the sand and wait for it all to get better. That is never going to happen, because as we all know nothing gets better if nothing changes. In fact, things often get worse.

Ignoring one's financial position is not the answer. Having someone by your side, ON your side, does help. Having a Spending Plan with Spending Made Easy will show you exactly where all of your financial commitments are going and will illustrate your financial future, before you get there! We leave no stone unturned. There is also no judgement and certainly no shaming. We have all made good and bad financial decisions in the past. The trick is to learn from them, draw a line under it all, and to move on. We deal with facts and the truths and we move forward. Following a Spending Plan is the focus we all need in our lives.

2. Accountability

Accountability works. We all know that, right? Ask anyone who has been on a weight loss journey and had to be weighed by a complete stranger on a regular basis. The fact that they are invested in you and keen to check up with you regularly, works!

If they show you what to do, guide you, encourage you and empower you, with all the tools you need to lose your weight, then you are more likely to stick to the weight loss program and thus lose the weight. You also know they are there for you if you have an "off day", or can't cope for any reason. Having a Spending Plan and a Spending Planner is exactly the same. Spending Made Easy check-up with you regularly and ensure you are on track to meet all your financial commitments and ultimately, your financial goals.

3. Teamwork

Much like the Accountability, when you have a Spending Planner in your corner, you have a team-mate. The Olympian who wins a gold medal at the Olympics does not get there alone. He/she has had a team guiding them, pushing them in the right direction. Giving all the support and encouragement they need to get the job done. The team are with them every step of the way, through the good times and the bad.

Having a Spending Planner is exactly the same. They are your team encouraging you along. They give you all the tools and support you need to ensure you know exactly what you are doing, and where you are going at any given time. If you slip up, or miss a "training session", they get you back on track and focussed in no time at all.

4. Expert Assistance

Question: Why would you pay someone to help you with your day-to-day finances if you haven't got much money to start off with? As I have mentioned earlier, not everyone is good at budgeting or organising their day-to-day finances. Particularly if you grew up at a time where you can have everything "now", and not have to pay for it until later. As we also know, budgeting isn't taught in schools and so is it no surprise that lots of people struggle?

If you aren't any good at Car Mechanics, you would not attempt to service or repair your car yourself. You would pay an expert.

If you were no good at painting and decorating, you would probably get an expert in to decorate, and you would pay that Decorator. It is just the same when you are seeking help with your day-to-day finances. Good quality help and support is not to be taken lightly and investing in your future is always a good investment. The real question should be, "Can you afford not to?".

5. Who needs a Spending Plan?

Who really needs to plan – aka use a Spending Plan? Everyone, that's who!

Typically, the more you earn, the more you spend! How many times have you gotten a pay-rise and it has just been swallowed up in the rest of your outgoings? Nothing really changed, did it?

Keeping track of your day-to-day spending, and more importantly, knowing what commitments are due in the future, is the way to go. A Spending Plan does all of this and more for you.

Spending Made Easy has many clients that we have helped over our many years in business and they range from a Young lady on purely benefits, to a wealthy young man earning in excess of $250,000 per annum, and everything in between.

One of the biggest struggles we see is that many people are spending exactly what they are earning, if not more. Yet if their pay halved for some reason, they would still manage.

Everyone needs a Spending Plan.

At this point, I would like you the reader, to reflect here. What is your spending behaviour and mindset like? How are your finances? Are they healthy, could they be healthier?

Please feel free to check out our website and arrange an appointment or feel free to take advantage of our DIY plan and start right away.

www.SpendingMadeEasy.com.au

Why A Spending Plan Is The Answer

Chapter 8

Do you live "pay cheque, to pay cheque" and stress over your day-to-day finances? Do you have your household Budget written on a piece of paper, or (even better) in a spreadsheet? Are you still arguing with your partner over money and have sleepless nights due to worrying about your financial future? Are you paying your bills on time, every time? Do you know where EVERY CENT of your hard-earned cash goes? Do you have "enough" savings, if any? Do you know how much "enough" savings are?

The list goes on...

Traditional Budgeting doesn't work. It deals with the "here and now" and often the historic. Times have changed. Nothing fits into the Budget anymore and so we put it all on credit, and the like. The Society we live in today allows us to indulge in all the things we want, as well as need, and it is leading to overspending and debt. Huge debt. We all want everything "now"; because we can have it now! Not very many of us think about the consequences of all the future repayments we are committing to; Credit Cards, Buy Now/Pay Later, and more…

A Spending Plan allows you to take control of YOUR OWN money and to pay your bills on time - every time, and with ease. You can see into your financial future and know exactly what payments are due and when, all very clear, in your very own Spending Plan. Once your Spending Plan is set up, all you have to do is, LIVE IT! You can see your financial future, right before your eyes. You even get to enjoy paying your bills!

You will sleep well at night and get more of what you want with less financial stress. It will take less time each week achieving all of those financial benefits that you never thought possible.

Spending Made Easy helps people get on track with their day-to-day finances. We teach you how to "set and forget" all of your regular financial commitments and get you saving for a fabulous and much brighter future. We also use awesome software that projects into the future for you, making your life even easier. Most importantly we have a proven track record of happy clients whose lives have changed for the better from our services.

"A Spending Plan is your financial compass. It shows you where you are, and where you need to go"

Samantha Boardman

The sooner we get going with your Spending Plan, the better you are at the end of the day, year, and decade! Contact us now to get started.

www.SpendingMadeEasy.com.au

Spending Made Easy: Success Stories

Chapter 9

The main reason we do what we do is the opportunity to help change the lives of people and their families. We love to help people that need help, and to also help themselves. If we can help people sleep better at night, not argue with their partner over money, reduce stress levels, and help them with their finances, then we see that as great success.

As I mentioned earlier in this book, I struggled a lot growing up and there was no help or support to guide me through. I had to cope with all of the financial commitments life threw at me, and continued to throw at me. I really wish I had a Spending Plan in my early 20s, or even sooner.

We have helped many people over the years; young and old, wealthy and not wealthy, males and females, couples and singles. You don't have to be financially struggling either to benefit from a Spending Plan, far from it.

Your own personal finances are often a delicate matter and so it is not everyone's cup of tea to share their financial situation. However, we are lucky enough to have some awesome clients that are very open with sharing their experience with us. Please allow me to share some of their stories here.

The very first client: Julian

Julian was a single father at the time. Who was struggling with his finances and needed a Spending Plan. This is what he had to say;

"The service is great for those people needing to sort out their finances and then learn to stay on track. The software lets you see where you are now and shows you where you will be in the future.

The best part about it all is the Spending Planner's enthusiasm and willingness to help. If she doesn't know an answer, there aren't many, she will find out for you. She is always available to help and does it all with a great sense of humour.

With their help I am now in a much better place and have learnt a lot about managing my money.

"Be accountable for your own spending. Look forward, not backwards"

Samantha Boardman

Thanks Spending Made Easy"

I will always be truly grateful to Julian for trusting me with my new business. He is still a client to this day and I affectionately call him my "Number 1 Client"; because he is.

Location is not an issue either, with video conferencing etc...

Luxemburg Lynsey

Lynsey lives in Luxembourg and we have helped her to become a financial master with her Spending Plan. This is what Lynsey had to say after 6 months with Spending Made Easy;

"I really needed this in my life. My circumstances changed but my mindset didn't. Luckily I found this before the situation descended too far. I am back on track and can monitor what I need to do so that I stay firmly within my Spending Plan.

Thanks Spending Made Easy"

The Convert

Paula was getting assistance from another budgeting organisation for 8 years. This is what she had to say after 6 months with Spending Made Easy;

"I was with ▓▓▓▓▓▓ *for close to 8 years, I got so sick of being asked to pay $5.50 to take out my own money because they forecasted 12 months in advance and that I never seemed to*

have surplus. I constantly had to call to make sure payments were being made on time and found out that my weekly costs to them had risen by $19 a week. It went from $29 to $48 over the years and they paid themselves first and foremost. And then by the grace of God I found Spending Made Easy, they have been my inspiration to take back control of my life and my finances and the software that runs it all is amazing and easy. I love easy. My Spending Planner is easy going and has a great sense of humour. What's more is that I'm feeling fantastic about the future and with Spending Made Easy's guidance and my shear determination I will prevail..."

We love helping people like Paula, as we have changed her life and helped her to regain control of her financial future.

The Beyond Help

This person initially thought and was convinced that she was beyond help. Eventually, she signed up with us and this was what she said after completing 6 months with us;

"I can't thank Spending Made Easy enough for the best service ever! I was sure that I was dire in my spending but my Spending Planner has gone above and beyond a consultant would and assured and helped me with my spending! Looking forward to having a few extra dollars in my pocket!

Thanks Spending Made Easy."

Unpredictable

Leanne and her husband both had fluctuating incomes and found it hard to account for future bills as they did not have a regular income. This is what Leanne had to say;

"I rate Spending Made Easy 5 stars as I haven't always been too good with money. I earn it and spend it. Budget is a dirty word. I can't tell you how grateful I am for meeting my Spending Planner, as she took me under her wing, and spent time showing me how I can save money. What I really liked about this is that I'm still in control. I don't have someone telling me I'm only allowed X amount. I have the say and so do you. When I fall off the wagon, my Spending Planner was always there to show me how to fix it. The very Best Part is the program shows me my balance a year in advance if I stay on track. I now have used this for the past 2 months and I can now start to look at booking my first overseas holiday in years. I seriously can't thank Spending Made Easy enough for giving me and my family the freedom we deserve. Thank you for everything, you are a real treasure."

Good Is Good, Better Is Better

Niki has always been good with her finances, she just wanted to be better! This is what she had to say;

"Spending Made Easy is Amazing!!!!!!! I now after years of juggling, have a clear plan in place to organise my finances, and continue experiencing life to the fullest!!!! I highly recommend anyone to have a chat with Spending Made Easy, so they can show you, how to turn your life around! Make that decision ASAP!!!!!!"

Niki is great and just wanted to be better around her finances. She just wanted to live her best life and have a Spending Plan in place to be more organised. She now enjoys her Jet Ski, Spending Plan and is saving for her next holiday.

The Heart Warmer

Chloe was a fabulous client and I often caught up with her and her Partner for our meetings. Her story makes my heart melt;

"My Spending Planner has made managing money so much easier. I know when everything is due and that I can afford all of my bills. Because of their help, my boyfriend and I are now planning a holiday. We know we can afford it. All thanks to Spending Made Easy."

Knowing these two lovely people went on holiday to Bali, after our help, is why we do it. Chloe even had her own spreadsheet open working alongside the Spending Plan. However, she knew that the spreadsheet was just not working and needed a change. That is why she got a Spending Plan, which revolutionised her habits and financial future.

One thing that we come across a lot is people saying that they wished they had signed up with Spending Made Easy sooner. Once they knew where all of their money was going, it opened their eyes to where they had made mistakes in the past, and then how to fix it. People also saw their financial future ahead of time and realised that they could squeeze stuff in they never thought possible! Such as Chloe's overseas holiday.

Why not take a holiday and plan ahead with a Spending Plan.

www.SpendingMadeEasy.com.au

Chapter 10

Spending Worksheet

The following worksheets are here for you to reflect on your current spending behaviours and to assist you to realise your full spending situation.

Using this completed worksheet, you can then evaluate how best to proceed and improve your financial life.

WANTS & NEEDS

List All Of Your Current WANTS That Costs You Money (these are things that if you didn't have you would still survive, e.g. luxury items, jewellery, beauty treatments, fancy cars)

Spending Worksheet

List All Of Your Current NEEDS That Costs You Money
(these are things that if you didn't have you would essentially die, e.g. shelter, food, water, etc...)

Prioritise Your Top 5 NEEDS In Order Of Importance

1.

2.

3.

4.

5.

Prioritise Your Top 5 WANTS In Order Of Importance

1.

2.

3.

4.

5.

Spending Worksheet

DREAMS & GOALS

What do you dream of doing and what are your goals? Is it study, go on holiday, buy a car, etc…? List your top 5.
1.
2.
3.
4.
5.
Out of the Top 5. What is the first one you would like to achieve?

WHAT DO YOU SPEND YOUR MONEY ON?

When filling out this sheet, make sure to include all of your dependents in the "spend per month". There is a separate section for children. If you are unsure of the exact amount of your "spend per month" an estimate can be used.

Home	Y/N	Spend Per Month
- Mortgage		
- Strata Fees		
- Home Repairs		
- Renovations		
- Rent		
- Electricity		
- Gas		
- Water		
- Rates		
- Insurances		
- Emergency Services Levy		
- Internet		
- Home Phone		
- Other		
	Total	

Spending Worksheet

Living	Y/N	Spend Per Month
- Food		
- Drinks (inc. alcohol)		
- Personal Mobile		
- Clothes		
- Sport/Clubs		
- Gym Membership		
- Medical/Medication		
- Dentist		
- Optometrist		
- Accountant		
- Bank Charges		
- Credit Card Fees		
- Hair cut/dressing		
- Pet food		
- Pet Medication		
- Pet Toys		
- Veterinary Bills		
Pet Other - - -		
Living Other - - -		
	Total	

Transport	Y/N	Spend Per Month
- Car (Purchase)		
- Mechanic/Repairs		
- Driver's Licence		
- Insurance		
- Parking		
- Fuel		
- Car Loan		
- Car Registration		
- Public Transport		
- Taxi/Ride Share		
- Passport		
- Airplane Tickets		
Other - - -		
	Total	

Spending Worksheet

Children	Y/N	Spend Per Month
- School Fees & Uniforms		
- Tutoring		
- Textbooks		
- Stationary & Backpack		
- Excursions		
- Clothes & Shoes		
- Medical/Medication		
- Toys		
Other - - -		
	Total	

Baby Care	Y/N	Spend Per Month
- Nappies/Diapers		
- Baby Food		
- Childcare		
- Medical/Medication		
- Toys		
- Clothes		
Other - - -		
	Total	

Leisure & Holiday	Y/N	Spend Per Month
- Cinema		
- Restaurants		
- Pub		
- Café		
- Tobacco		
- Newspapers/Magazines		
- Online Subscriptions		
- Charitable Donations		
- Presents/Gifts		
- Airplane Tickets		
- Transport		
- Hotels		
- Cruise Tickets		
- Further Education Fees		
Other - - -		
	Total	

SPENDING SUMMARY PAGE

Home	
Total	

Living	
Total	

Transport	
Total	

Children	
Total	

Baby Care	
Total	

Leisure & Holiday	
Total	

Add all of the totals together.

GRAND SPENDING TOTAL _____ per month **(A)**

HOW MUCH DO YOU EARN A MONTH?

I earn _____ per month, after tax. **(B)**

HOW MUCH DO YOU HAVE LEFT OVER?

(B)	-	(A)	=	(C)
Earnings per month		Spending per month		Left over per month

YOUR VALUE OF C

Did you get a Positive Number?

If you got a positive number, then you are a **Healthy Spender**. Well done You! You have more coming in than going out, which is an awesome position to be in. However, what are you doing with that excess money and would you like to increase it? There is always room for improvement. Everyone has hopes and dreams with their money. It is time to take action, and to plan for the future. Tweak a few things here and there, and see what you can achieve. Challenge yourself to increase your number with a Spending Plan! Exciting times are ahead.

Did you get Zero?

If you got a zero, then good on you. You are a **Balanced Spender**. This means your incomings match your outgoings. However, do you have a rainy-day fund? Emergency fund? Any Savings? Take a good look at everything, especially your outgoings. Perhaps a bit of tweaking will push you into having a positive number, then you can really start to plan! Get a Spending Plan and try making a few changes. See how you go. You may be surprised at what you can achieve. Good Luck!

Did you get a Negative Number?

If you got a negative number then you are an **Unbalanced Spender**. You have more going out than coming in, which is not the best position to be in. You need to take a good look at what you do have going out and cut back accordingly as you will run out of money and any savings you do have will go backwards. This situation is not as alarming as you might first think as a Spending Plan can help.

Get a Spending Plan and learn what might be good to cut back on. You can also learn to prepare for any unexpected expenses. It can make a huge difference. Getting a Spending Plan sooner, rather than later, is the best thing to do in order to become a **Healthy Spender**. Furthermore, once you are a healthy spender we can start working on realising your dream goals in life.

It is important to note too, that often people think that they are an Unbalanced Spender, when in fact a Spending Plan proves to them, that they are indeed, a Healthy Spender! At Spending Made Easy, we see this situation time and time again. Are you one of those people? How do you even know for sure? Contact us to find out.

Spending Worksheet

Get a Spending Plan from Spending Made Easy.

www.SpendingMadeEasy.com.au

www.ingramcontent.com/pod-product-compliance
Lightning Source LLC
Chambersburg PA
CBHW072102290426
44110CB00014B/1790